# FUNFAX™

# BREEDS

Written by Joanne Bednall

...ographers for their kind
...: Robert Oliver and Bob
...rses and ponies: Percheron -
...De L'isue Briano, France.
...Kentucky Horse Park, USA.
Trakehner - Horse: ........., ........mayer, Germany. Fell Pony -
Pony: Heltondale Daisy III; Owner: K.A. and S.B.M. Feakins, Hereford.
Shagya Arab - Horse: Artaxerxes; Owner: Jeanette Bauch & Jens Brinksten,
Denmark. Lusitano - Horse: Montemere-O-Nova (Romano); Owner: Nan
Thurman, Turville Valley Stud, Oxon. French Trotter - Horse: Pur Historien;
Owner: Haras National De Compiegne, France. Orlov Trotter - Owner:
Moscow Hippodrome, USSR. Irish Draught - Horse: Miss Mill. Oldenburgh -
Horse: Renoir ( Modelkonig); Owner: Louise Tomkins. Pinto - Horse: Hit
Man; Owner: Boyd Cantrell, Kentucky Horse Park, USA. Palomino - Horse:
Wychwood Dynascha; Owner: Mrs G. Harwood, Wychwood Stud,
Glos. Ariégeois - Horse: Radium; Owner: Haras National De Tarbes,
France. Falabella - Horse: Pegasus of Kilverstone; Owner Lady Fisher,
Kilverstone Wildlife Park, Norfolk. Exmoor Pony - Pony: Murrayton
Delphinus; Owner: June Freeman, Murrayton Stud, Herts. Welsh Pony -
Pony: Twyford Signal; Owner: Mr and Mrs L.E. Bigley, Llanarth Stud,
Hereford. Dales Pony - Pony: Warrendale Duke; Owner: Mr Dickson,
Millbeck Pony Stud, Yorks. Connemara Pony - Pony: Spinway Bright
Morning; Owner: Miss S. Hodgkins, Spinway Stud, Oxon. Clydesdale -
Horse: Blue Print; Owner: Mervyn and Pauline Ramage, Mount Farm
Clydesdale Horses, Tyne and Wear. Ardennais - Horse: Ramses Du Vallon;
Haras National De Pau, France. Polo Pony - Horse: Basarita; Owner: Turf
and Travel, Eton High Street, London. Hack - Horse: Rye Tangle;
Owner: Robert Oliver.

# FUNFAX™

A Funfax Book
First published in Great Britain by Funfax Ltd.,
an imprint of Dorling Kindersley Limited,
9 Henrietta Street, London WC2E 8PS
Copyright © 1999 Funfax Ltd.

# COAT COLOURS

The modern horse evolved from a creature the size of a dog around 60 million years ago. Now, with more than 160 equine breeds and types around the world, it's not surprising that horses and ponies come in a variety of colours, shades and patterns. Here are the ten main types...

## Bay
Reddish-brown coat with black mane, tail and legs (called 'points').

## Black
True blacks have a black coat, skin and muzzle.

## Brown
A chocolate-brown coat, mane, tail and legs.

## Chestnut
Coats range from gold-, yellow- or reddish-brown to liver (dark).

## Coloured
Piebalds have black-and-white patches; skewbalds (right) have white with another colour (usually brown); odd-coloured horses are white with two or more colours.

# COAT COLOURS

## Dun
Dull yellow hairs with a dark mane, tail, legs and often a dorsal (eel) stripe along the spine. Yellow duns are creamy-yellow and blue duns are greyish-black.

## Grey
Light greys (right) have more white hairs than black; 'flea-bitten' greys have dark flecks on a 'white' coat; dapple greys have rings of dark hairs forming a mottled pattern; iron greys have more black hairs than white, giving a blue-grey tint.

## Palomino
A golden coat three shades lighter or darker than a newly-minted gold coin. The mane and tail are always white.

## Roan
Strawberry roans (right) have chestnut and white hairs, giving a pinkish tinge; blue roans have white hairs mixed with black or brown hairs.

## Spotted
Usually when dark spots cover a white base.

# AKHAL-TEKE

- **Place of origin:** Turkmenistan, central Asia
- **Height:** 15-16 hh
- **Colours:** bay, chestnut, black, grey and dun, often with a stunning metallic sheen
- **Characteristics:** bold, intelligent, fast and strong-willed. Can survive intense heat and days without water

## History

This unusual-looking desert horse is said to be at least 4,000 years old. As far back as 500 BC, Akhal-Tekes were used as war mounts, but they earned their reputation as the greyhound of the horse world long before this.

## Uses

Today, the breed is still valued for racing and long-distance riding. In fact, no other horse can match its endurance and stamina. On top of this, the Akhal-Teke is also proving itself at dressage and showjumping.

## Fascinating Fact

In 1935, Akhal-Tekes covered an amazing 4,152 km (2,580 miles) from Ashkhabad, in Turkmenistan, to Moscow, in Russia. Travelling in blistering heat during the daytime, and enduring freezing night-time temperatures, they also went without water for much of the 84-day journey.

# ANDALUCIAN

- **Place of origin:** Spain
- **Height:** 15.2 hh
  **Colours:** bay, grey and black
- **Characteristics:** agile, spirited, intelligent, strong, courageous and docile

## History

It's thought that the Andalucian developed from primitive native ponies breeding with North African Barb horses brought to Spain by the Muslim invaders in 711 AD.

## Uses

For years, this noble horse has been the favourite mount of the Spanish 'rejoneadore' (bullfighter) because of its agility, balance and prancing action. Its spectacular paces also make it ideal for high school work (moves of the Spanish Riding School in Vienna) and competitive driving. Andalucians play an important and popular part in Spain's traditional festivals and parades.

## Fascinating Fact

In the 17th and 18th centuries, the breed was nearly ruined when attempts were made to increase its size. Thankfully, the Andalucian's purity was preserved by Carthusian monks, whose stud at their monastery in Jerez still stands today.

# APPALOOSA

- **Place of origin:** America
- **Height:** usually 14.2-15.2 hh
- **Colours:** the five basic spotted coat patterns are leopard, blanket, snowflake, few spot and marble
- **Characteristics:** athletic, agile, willing, hardy, versatile and kind, with endless stamina and endurance

## History

The Nez Percé Indians of northeast Oregon developed the Appaloosa by breeding spotted Spanish horses imported by the 'conquistadores' (invaders). It wasn't long before the breed was modelling a range of colourful coat patterns and proving itself as the perfect mount for war and hunting.

## Uses

It seems that there's no end to this eye-catching horse's talents. It's used on ranches, as a general riding horse, for jumping and racing, and in parades and circuses.

## Fascinating Fact

Ancestors of the Appaloosa appear in cave drawings created by early man 20,000 years ago.

# ARAB

- **Place of origin:** Arabian Peninsula, The Middle East
- **Height:** ideally 14.2-15 hh
- **Colours:** black, bay, grey and chestnut
- **Characteristics:** spirited, intelligent, courageous and sound, with a gentle nature, stamina and endurance

## History

Existing on the Arabian Peninsula since around 2,500 BC, this beautiful desert horse's purity was protected by Bedouins (desert travellers) for more than 1,000 years. In fact, according to legend, the god Allah created the Arab out of a handful of the south wind.

## Uses

Arabs can't compete with Thoroughbreds for speed or jumping ability, yet few breeds can match its endurance. That's why it excels at long-distance riding events worldwide.

## Fascinating Fact

Napoleon had his own stud of Arab horses. He rode his favourite grey Arab charger, Marengo, into battle at Waterloo in 1815.

# BARB

- **Place of origin:** Morocco, North Africa
- **Height:** 14.2-15.2 hh
- **Colours:** black, brown, bay and grey
- **Characteristics:** very fast over short distances, tough, agile, courageous, docile and sound, with excellent stamina and endurance

## History

The Barb's true history is a mystery, but it could have come from a small herd of wild horses which escaped the Ice Age. During the Muslim conquests in the 7th and 8th centuries, Barbs were crossed with Arabs and ridden by the Berbers when they invaded Spain.

## Uses

The 'plain Jane' looks of the Barb cunningly disguise its many talents. It is used as a cavalry mount, and is able to live on small amounts of poor food and survive intense heat and drought.

## Fascinating Fact

The primitive Barb may have been underrated for centuries but its importance has now become recognised. Many of the world's breeds, including the striking Andalucian, have this desert horse to thank for their development.

# CAMARGUE

- **Place of origin:** France
- **Height:** around 14 hh
- **Colour:** white
- **Characteristics:** hardy, fiery, courageous, sure-footed, intelligent, agile, active and generous, with great stamina

## History

This breed has probably lived in the marshy, harsh environment of the Rhône delta since at least 15,000 BC, when horses resembling Camargues were drawn on cave walls. It owes its primitive appearance to the Barb, which was introduced in the 7th and 8th centuries by the Moorish invaders, but has otherwise remained pure for the last 1,000 years or so.

## Uses

The equine equivalent of a sheepdog, the Camargue is used by France's cowboys, the 'gardians', to round up the black bulls of the Rhône delta region.

## Fascinating Fact

Visitors come from far and wide to see the famous semi-wild herds, known as 'manades'. So it's no wonder that these sure-footed 'white horses of the sea' are becoming increasingly popular for carrying tourists around the area.

# CASPIAN

- **Place of origin:** Iran
- **Height:** 10-12 hh
- **Colours:** bay, chestnut, grey, roan, black and a rare light red dun, often with a metallic sheen
- **Characteristics:** intelligent, sharp, fast and agile

## History
Just when equine experts were sure that the Caspian had been as dead as a dodo for 1,000 years, up popped a small oriental horse on the shores of Iran's Caspian Sea in 1965. Discovered by American Louise Firouz, the animal turned out to be a Caspian. Others were found and further research showed that the breed might even be older than the Arab.

## Uses
During the Iran-Iraq war of the 1980s, this rare breed was used to detect mines. It is now popular for driving and as a children's showjumper.

## Fascinating Fact
Although the Caspian is a miniature horse, it can match its bigger cousins stride-for-stride, except at the gallop – the bones in its legs look more like they belong to a wild ass!

# CLYDESDALE

- **Place of origin:** Scotland
- **Height:** 16.2-17 hh
- **Colours:** bay, brown, grey, black and roan
- **Characteristics:** active, brave and friendly

## History

This huge horse's history can be traced back to the 18th century, when farmers crossed their hardy local mares with heavier imported Flemish stallions. It is possible that the Clydesdale contains some Shire blood, too.

## Uses

Despite the Clydesdale weighing up to 1 tonne, it remains an elegant, high-stepping breed, popular for hauling brewery drays and for pulling work in cities, forests, prairies and farms around the world. The Clydesdale is popular in America, Canada, Germany, the former USSR, South Africa, Australia, New Zealand and Japan.

## Fascinating Fact

In 1990, an 18.2 hh colt was sold to a Japanese buyer for an incredible £20,000. A big price for a big fellow!

# CONNEMARA

- **Place of origin:** County Galway, Ireland
- **Height:** 13-14.2 hh
- **Colours:** black, bay, brown, grey, dun, chestnut, palomino, roan and cream
- **Characteristics:** courageous, fast, sensible and hardy

## History
In the 16th and 17th centuries, Galway's traders crossed local ponies with Barbs and Spanish horses to produce the now-extinct Irish Hobby. Hobbies, Welsh Cobs, Arabs, Thoroughbreds, Roadsters, Hackneys, Irish Draughts and Clydesdales all played their part in developing the Connemara.

## Uses
Connemaras excel at showjumping, dressage and showing, especially when crossed with the Thoroughbred. Legendary Irish showjumper Dundrum, Olympic dressage horse Little Model and 1973 Badminton Three-Day Event runner-up Eagle Rock, all had Connemara blood.

## Fascinating Fact
For centuries, Connemaras were used to carry peat, corn, potatoes and seaweed. Now they are international stars!

 **DALES**

- **Place of origin:** eastern Pennines, England
- **Height:** up to 14.2 hh
- **Colours:** mainly black but sometimes bay, brown and grey (rare)
- **Characteristics:** sensible, calm, very strong, sure-footed, courageous and healthy, with good stamina

## History

Larger and heavier than its cousin the Fell, this pony has the black Friesian, the now-extinct Galloway pony, the high-stepping Welsh Cob and the heavy Clydesdale to thank for its development.

### Uses

Due to their immense strength, Dales ponies were used during the 18th and 19th centuries to power machinery in mines, and to carry loads of lead ore and coal to the seaports. They also worked on farms, performed general pack duties, and pulled carts and carriages – but not all at the same time! Nowadays, the Dales is in demand for trekking and driving.

## Fascinating Fact

The Dales pony can carry loads well out of proportion to its size – up to 100 kg (220 lb).

# DARTMOOR

- **Place of origin:** Devon, England
- **Height:** up to 12.2 hh
- **Colours:** bay, black and brown
- **Characteristics:** kind, sensible, sure-footed, sound and hardy

## History
Originally, the early moorland ponies were rather rough and ready. But not today's Dartmoor. A multitude of breeds, including Arabs and Thoroughbreds, were used in the 19th century to upgrade the Dartmoor.

## Uses
The Dartmoor is used as an elegant children's riding pony, and is at home both in the showjumping ring and the showing arena.

## Fascinating Fact
During World War II, the breed came close to extinction because the army used Dartmoor as a training centre. Luckily, a handful of dedicated breeders came to the rescue and started to increase the number of purebreds.

# EXMOOR

- **Place of origin:** Somerset, England
- **Height:** 12.2-12.3 hh
- **Colours:** bay, brown or dun, often with a metallic sheen in summer
- **Characteristics:** hardy, fast, very strong, well balanced and nervous; Exmoors are especially afraid of strangers and dogs

## History
Exmoor's harsh habitat has been responsible for keeping Britain's oldest mountain and moorland breed pure for centuries. In fact, fossil bones from the Exmoor's ancestors date back to the Ice Age, a mind-blowing 100,000 years ago.

## Uses
In the Bronze Age, the breed was used to pull chariots, but today it is a popular children's riding pony. The Exmoor is well known for its jumping and galloping ability – the 1869 and 1870 Grand National winner, The Colonel, had Exmoor blood.

## Fascinating Fact
Now a registered rare and endangered breed, it's estimated there are only 1,000 purebred Exmoors left worldwide.

# FALABELLA

- **Place of origin:** Argentina
- **Height:** under 85 cm (34 in); ideally around 75 cm (30 in)
- **Colours:** all colours, but spotted coats are more in demand
- **Characteristics:** friendly, agile, athletic and intelligent

## History

Lots of good things come in small packages, including the world's smallest horse, the Falabella. This pint-sized breed was founded by the Falabella family, who crossed a Shetland pony with a very small Thoroughbred at their ranch in Argentina about a century ago.

## Uses

Although the Falabella is too small to be ridden, it performs well in harness and at in-hand showjumping. It is also a popular pet, especially in America.

## Fascinating Fact

One of the smallest Falabellas was an American mare called Sugar Dumpling, who stood only 50 cm (20 in) high and weighed an ultra-light 13.5 kg (30 lb).

# FELL

- **Place of origin:** north Pennines, England
- **Height:** up to 14 hh
- **Colours:** black, brown, bay and grey
- **Characteristics:** hardy, strong, sure-footed, intelligent, courageous and alert, with good stamina and endurance and a nice temperament

## History

The breed evolved from black Friesians brought to Britain by the Romans, and fast Galloway ponies.

## Uses

The Fell was used during the 17th and 18th centuries for transporting heavy loads of lead from the northern mines to the coast. Smaller and lighter than its Dales cousin over the hills, the Fell has since left its pack-carrying and farm-working image behind and is now in great demand for riding and driving.

## Fascinating Fact

This terrific trotter is a favourite of HRH the Duke of Edinburgh, who competes a team of four in carriage driving events.

# FJORD

- **Place of origin:** Norway
- **Height:** 13-14 hh
- **Colours:** various shades of dun with a dorsal (eel) stripe running along its spine and often zebra markings on the legs
- **Characteristics:** powerful, sure-footed, courageous, hard-working, gentle, strong-minded and long-lived, with lots of stamina and endurance

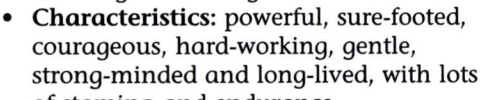

## History

The Fjord originated in Norway as a Viking horse used in horse-fighting. When the Vikings and their ponies with strange 'punk' manes arrived on Scottish soil more than 1,000 years ago, they must have been a frightening sight.

## Uses

This gentle and hard-working pony became valued in its native Norway for agricultural and forestry work, carrying packs and pleasure riding. Today, the breed is still preferred to tractors on some farms, but its main claim to fame is winning long-distance riding and competitive driving events.

## Fascinating Fact

It is a tradition to clip a Fjord pony's mane so that it stands up like a spiky haircut!

# HAFLINGER

- **Place of origin:** Austria
- **Height:** up to 13.3 hh
- **Colour:** chestnut with a flaxen (creamy yellow) mane and tail
- **Characteristics:** sound, hardy, kind, versatile, hard-working, willing, sure-footed and long-lived

## History
All purebred Haflingers can trace their roots to the breed's founding stallion, the Arab, EL Bedavi XXII, in the 19th century. The now-extinct Alpine Heavy Horse and other local breeds have also contributed to the Haflinger. Raised on alpine pastures, where the thin mountain air develops its heart and lungs, it's no surprise that the Haflinger can live to a great age – some are still fit and active at 40!

## Uses
One of the world's most attractive ponies, the breed draws sleighs, pulls carts and carriages, works in forests and on farms, and is excellent for all-round riding and driving.

## Fascinating Fact
All Haflingers bred at Austria's main Jenesien Stud bear a brand featuring the country's national flower, the edelweiss, with the letter 'H' in the middle.

# HANOVERIAN

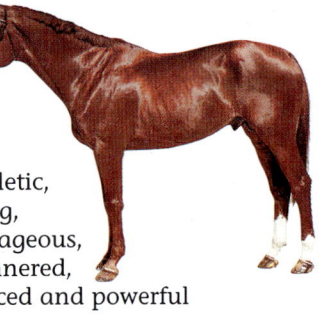

- **Place of origin:** Germany
- **Height:** 15.3-16.2 hh
- **Colours:** all solid colours
- **Characteristics:** athletic, agile, reliable, willing, kind, energetic, courageous, intelligent, well mannered, versatile, well balanced and powerful

## History
Founded at a German stud in 1735 by King George II, the Hanoverian is based on Holsteins with Thoroughbred and Trakehner blood, and is the best-known of the European warmbloods. It descends from the famous Hanoverian Creams, which were used as carriage horses for ceremonial occasions in Germany. They were used for British royal processions until King George V's reign, when they were replaced by the Windsor Greys.

## Uses
The Hanoverian has earned a worldwide reputation as a top-class showjumper and dressage horse.

## Fascinating Fact
Not only is this breed rather talented and good looking, but it has a winning personality with a price tag to match! Studs and breeders consider a kind temperament as important as correct conformation (shape) and athleticism.

# HIGHLAND

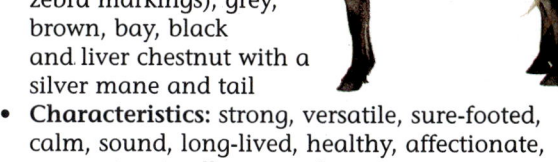

- **Place of origin:** Scotland
- **Height:** up to 14.2 hh
- **Colours:** dun (with an eel stripe and sometimes zebra markings), grey, brown, bay, black and liver chestnut with a silver mane and tail
- **Characteristics:** strong, versatile, sure-footed, calm, sound, long-lived, healthy, affectionate, responsive, intelligent and sensitive

## History

The Highland has been around for a very long time. Its ancestors lived in northern Scotland and the Scottish islands after the Ice Age. In the 17th and 18th centuries, native ponies were crossed with Spanish horses and an early type of Percheron. An Arab and other breeds were introduced in the 19th century.

## Uses

Previously popular as a pack pony and farm and forestry worker, today's multi-purpose Highland has grown into the perfect family pony. It is ideal for trekking, jumping and driving.

## Fascinating Fact

The Highland pony has a long history. In France, there are 15-20,000-year-old cave drawings of ponies fitting the breed's description.

# ICELANDIC

- **Place of origin:** Iceland
- **Height:** 12.3-13.2 hh
- **Colours:** dun, grey, bay, black, chestnut (often with a flaxen mane and tail), palomino, albino, piebald and skewbald
- **Characteristics:** strong, hardy, agile, sure-footed, docile and friendly, cheap and easy to keep

## History

Norwegian immigrants first introduced ponies to Iceland, a land of lava and glaciers, around the end of the 9th century. In 930 AD, Iceland's parliament passed laws banning the import of other breeds, ensuring that the Icelandic has remained pure.

## Uses

The Icelandic plays an important part in the past and present of its isolated homeland and the people who live there. These ponies are used for work, pleasure and sport, including dressage, cross-country and racing.

## Fascinating Fact

The Icelandic has five gaits: 'fetgangur' (walk) for pack-carrying, 'brokk' (trot) for crossing rough country, 'skeid' (pace) for covering short distances at speed, 'tölt' (running walk) for accelerating over broken ground and 'stökk' (fast gallop).

# IRISH DRAUGHT

- **Place of origin:** Ireland
- **Height:** 16-17 hh
- **Colours:** bay, brown, chestnut and grey
- **Characteristics:** even tempered, sensible, healthy, willing, strong, athletic, agile and bold

## History

Today's handsome and talented Irish Draught has evolved from a mixture of Spanish, French and Flemish horses imported into Ireland from the time of the Anglo-Norman invasion of 1172.

## Uses

Until World War II, the breed was in demand as a military and draught horse. Now, with their natural jumping ability, Irish Draughts make popular hunters and all-round riding horses. If you cross a Thoroughbred with an Irish Draught, you get an Irish Hunter, which is said to be the world's best cross-country horse.

## Fascinating Fact

After World War II, numbers of purebred Irish Draughts fell to an all-time low of less than 100. Luckily, thanks to the Rare Breeds Survival Trust and the Irish Draught Horse Society, it is no longer on the danger list.

# LIPIZZANER

- **Place of origin:** Lipizza, now in Slovenia
- **Height:** 15.1-16.2 hh
- **Colours:** mainly white but sometimes bay
- **Characteristics:** intelligent, willing, obedient, agile, athletic, quiet-natured and long-lived

## History

The Lipizzaner was founded in 1580 from Spanish mares and stallions. Other breeds such as the Kladruber, an Arab and the now extinct Neopolitan were added over the next 200 years or so.

## Uses

Lipizzaners are famous as the dancing white horses of Vienna's Spanish Riding School. Stunning Lipizzaner stallions thrill visitors at the world's oldest riding academy with their advanced movements. They show off tricky steps such as 'piaffe' (trotting on the spot), 'passage' (slow motion trot), pirouette and the difficult 'airs' above the ground, such as the 'capriole' ('leap of the goat'). Lipizzaners also make excellent carriage and riding horses. They enjoy a long life – many still perform demanding exercises into their 20s and some live to over 30.

## Fascinating Fact

Lipizzaner foals are born black or brown but grow up to be white.

# NEW FOREST

- **Place of origin:** Hampshire, England
- **Height:** 12-14.2 hh
- **Colours:** any, except piebald, skewbald and blue-eyed cream
- **Characteristics:** sure-footed, easily handled, strong, quick to learn and versatile

## History

There have been ponies living and breeding in Hampshire's New Forest since 1016. This was a busy trade route, so Forest ponies bred freely. Over the next several hundred years, Welsh ponies, Thoroughbreds, Arabs owned by Queen Victoria, many of Britain's native ponies and even a South African Basuto pony were used to upgrade the breed. Despite this variety of blood, the New Forest has developed its own individual character, action and appearance.

## Uses

This breed is a safe, good all-round children's riding pony, excelling at cross-country. New Forests are also strong enough to carry adults.

## Fascinating Fact

New Forest ponies have no fear of traffic, and often walk along roadside verges in the hope of being fed by tourists – something that is not encouraged.

# PERCHERON

- **Place of origin:** France
- **Height:** 15.2-17 hh
- **Colours:** grey, black and occasionally bay, chestnut and roan
- **Characteristics:** powerful, hardy, versatile, energetic, docile, easy to handle and intelligent

## History

The Percheron, having been influenced by Arab blood from as early as the 8th century, possesses many favourable attributes – it is handsome, elegant, popular and intelligent. The breed's long, free, low and stylish action has added to its worldwide appeal. It's popular as far afield as North and South America, South Africa, Australia, Japan and the Falkland Islands.

## Uses

As well as proving itself as a warhorse, especially on the battlefields of World War I, Percherons have excelled as coach, farm and gun horses.

## Fascinating Fact

An Australian Percheron mare holds the unofficial pulling record of 1,548 kg (3,412 lb), while the American Percheron, Dr Le Gear, is the world's largest horse, standing at a massive 21 hh.

# QUARTER HORSE

- **Place of origin:**
  America
- **Height:**
  14.3-16 hh
- **Colours:**
  all solid colours
- **Characteristics:**
  strong, fast, agile
  and well balanced

## History

The Quarter Horse is American through and through. It was developed in the early 17th century from Spanish stock, Barbs, Arabs and horses brought over by English settlers. The equine equivalent of a human 100-metre sprinter, the Quarter Horse is quick and muscular. It is said to be the world's most popular horse with the most extensive breed registry.

## Uses

Early Quarter Horses proved useful for farm work, herding cattle, hauling timber, light harness work and riding. The breed was also raced over quarter-mile stretches, and is the fastest horse in the world over this distance. Today, the Quarter Horse is used in rodeos, on the racetrack, as a trail mount and on ranches.

## Fascinating Fact

Quarter Horses have had starring roles in such films as *Black Beauty*, *The Horse Whisperer* and *Dances With Wolves*.

# SHETLAND

- **Place of origin:** Shetland Islands, Scotland
- **Height:** around 1.1 m (42 in)
- **Colours:** black, brown, chestnut, grey, piebald and skewbald
- **Characteristics:** courageous, sure-footed, hardy, strong, easy to train and adaptable

## History

It's thought that ancestors of this tiny pony arrived on the Shetland Islands from Scandinavia 10,000 years ago.

## Uses

On its bleak and gale-swept homeland 161 km (100 miles) off the north coast of Scotland, the Shetland has been valued for centuries as a pack animal, carrying seaweed and fetching peat for fuel. In the mid-19th century, Shetlands were used as pit ponies. Nowadays, they are popular in harness, for circus work and as children's riding ponies. The final of the Shetland Pony Grand National at London's Olympia Showjumping Championships is always highly competitive but great fun.

## Fascinating Fact

It may be the smallest of Britain's mountain and moorland breeds, but the Shetland is the strongest horse in the world relative to its size.

 **SHIRE**

- **Place of origin:** Midland counties of England
- **Height:** 16.2-17.2 hh
- **Colours:** black, bay, brown and grey
- **Characteristics:** strong, gentle, kind, docile, active, adaptable, hard-working and enduring

## History

The breed descends from England's medieval warhorse, the Great Horse, or English Black as it was called by the General and Statesman, Oliver Cromwell. It was the only horse strong enough to carry a fully armoured knight into battle. During the 16th and 17th centuries, Flemish horses and Friesians were used to upgrade the breed.

### Uses

Before World War II, the Shire was the main means of power for agriculture and industry, but its popularity fell after 1945 with increased mechanisation. Numbers have since been boosted by brewery companies, who still use Shires to pull their drays (carts).

## Fascinating Fact

This gentle giant is many people's idea of a heavy horse. The Shire can weigh more than 1 tonne and exceed 18 hh.

# THOROUGHBRED

- **Place of origin:** England
- **Height:** about 15.2-16.2 hh
- **Colours:** brown, bay chestnut, black and grey
- **Characteristics:** bold, active and courageous, with great stamina – can be highly-strung, nervous and sensitive

## History
The breed evolved in Britain in the 17th and 18th centuries from Arabs, now-extinct Scottish Galloways, Irish Hobbies and Spanish and Italian imports. The three foundation stallions are the Byerley Turk, the Darley Arabian and the Godolphin Arabian. Flying Childers was the first great racehorse.

## Uses
The Thoroughbred is used for flat and jump racing. Thoroughbred racing is a multi-million pound industry all over the world. The Thoroughbred is also a runaway success at showjumping, dressage and cross-country.

## Fascinating Fact
The Thoroughbred is the fastest, most valuable and most graceful horse in the world.

# TRAKEHNER

- **Place of origin:** East Prussia, now Lithuania
- **Height:** 16-16.2 hh
- **Colours:** all solid colours
- **Characteristics:** good natured, athletic, agile, active, loyal, courageous and intelligent, with great endurance and stamina

## History
Trakehners evolved from 13th century plain Schweiken ponies, with Thoroughbreds and Arabs being added 600 years later. In 1732, The Royal Trakehnen Stud was founded by King Friedrich Wilheim I of Prussia. It produced elegant and speedy coach horses and quality army chargers.

## Uses
Claimed to be Europe's perfect all-round competition horse, the Trakehner is equally talented at dressage, showjumping and cross-country.

## Fascinating Fact
During World War II, 800 Trakehners were trekked 965 km (600 miles) across war-torn Europe to avoid capture by the Russians. Less than 100 survived, but these founded today's Trakehner.

- **Place of origin:**
  Wales
- **Height:**
  Section A – up to 12 hh
  Section B – up to 13.2 hh
  Section D – up to 15 hh
- **Colours:** grey, palomino,
  bay, chestnut, roan and dun
- **Characteristics:**
  Sections A & B – intelligent,
  tough, sound, courageous and high-spirited
  Section D – courageous, sure-footed,
  sound, easy to manage, cheap to keep,
  bold, energetic and intelligent

## Section A

The Welsh Mountain Pony is the smallest of Wales's breeds and possibly the most beautiful pony in the world. Native stock was improved by the Romans' oriental horses, followed in the 18th and 19th centuries by Arabs, Thoroughbreds and Hackneys. Today, it is popular worldwide for driving and as a children's riding and show pony.

## Section B

The slightly bigger Welsh Pony is the world's most talented harness, competition, riding and show pony.

## Section D

The Welsh Cob (shown above) is a larger version of Section A. It excels at competitive driving, hunting and jumping.